DOES THE CRITICAL TEXT CONTAIN DOCTRINAL ERRORS?

A PowerPoint Presentation by Dr. D. A. Waite

				D	O	C	T	R	I	N	E			
					R			E						
		T	E	X	T	U	A	L						
		R			H			A						
E	Q	U	I	V	O	C	A	T	E					
		T			D			I						
		H			O			V	A	R	I	A	N	T
					X			E						
					Y			L						
								Y						

Wayside Baptist Church

Greenville, SC

September 26, 2009

Published by

THE BIBLE FOR TODAY PRESS

900 Park Avenue
Collingswood, New Jersey 08108
U.S.A.

Church Phone: 856-854-4747

BFT Phone: 856-854-4452

Orders: 1-800-John 10:9

email: BFT@BibleForToday.org

Website:www.BibleForToday.org

Fax: 856-854-2464

$8.00 + $5.00 S&H

We Use and Defend
the King James Bible

September, 2009

BFT #3418

TABLE OF CONTENTS
"Does the Critical Text Contain Doctrinal Errors?"

I. **Introductory Matters** 1
   A. **Why This Bible Conference** 1
   B. **The General Topic** 1
   C, **Why This Topic Today** 1
   D. **The Specific Topic** 1
      1. **Definitions of terms** 1
      2. **Rephrasing the Specific Topic** 2
II. **Introducing the BJU Teachers Making False Statements on Doctrine** . 3
   A. **BJU Teacher Dr. Mark Minnick** 3
   B. **BJU Teacher Dr. Samuel Schnaiter** 3
III. **The Sources for These Quotations** 3
   A. **The Sources for Dr. Minnick's Quotes** 3
   B. **The Sources for Dr. Schnaiter's Quotes** 5
IV. **The Four Quotations From Dr. Mark Minnick** 5
   A. **Quote #1** 5
   B. **Quote #2** 8
   C. **Quote #3** 10
   D. **Quote #4** 14
V. **The Thirteen Quotations from Dr. Samuel Schnaiter** 17
   A. **Quote #1** 18
   A. **Quote #2** 19
   A. **Quote #3** 21
   A. **Quote #4** 24
   A. **Quote #5** 26
   A. **Quote #6** 27
   A. **Quote #7** 29
   A. **Quote #8** 31
   A. **Quote #9** 34
   A. **Quote #10** 36
   A. **Quote #11** 38
   A. **Quote #12** 40
   A. **Quote #13** 42
V. **Conclusions and Other Important Definitions** 45
BOOKS & MATERIALS FOR FURTHER STUDY 48

Why This Bible Conference?

Outline of The Conference (#1)

I. Pastor Kenneth Rainey has given the background of the Bible Conference, giving the reasons for it and describing the original debate topic "RESOLVED THAT THE CRITICAL TEXT CONTAINS DOCTRINAL ERRORS." He has read the invitations to BJU teachers, Dr. Samuel Schnaiter and Dr. Mark Minnick as well as their responses.

1

Why This Bible Conference?

Outline of The Conference (#2)

II. Pastor Rainey invited two men to help him reply to the original debate topic, by quoting, and then answering, the two BJU teachers.

A. Pastor D. A. Waite, Th.D., Ph.D. from Collingswood, NJ, will present the Power Point series.

B. Dr. H. D. Williams, M.D., Ph.D. from Cleveland, GA, will assist him with the video projection and will contribute to the question and answer periods.

2

The General Topic Today

The general topic today concerns the <u>Critical Greek Text</u> that underlies modern Bible versions.

It is <u>limited</u> to the area of the <u>DOCTRINAL ERRORS</u> contained in that Critical Greek Text."

3

Why This Topic Today?

The following title was the debate topic sent to these two Bob Jones University teachers.

We wish they had agreed to come and defend some very false statements made in their books to the effect that the Critical Greek Text does not contain any doctrinal errors.

We believe these statements should be refuted factually and clearly.

4

The Original Debate Resolution

"RESOLVED THAT THE <u>CRITICAL TEXT</u> CON-TAINS <u>DOCTRINAL ER-RORS</u>."

5

The Original Debate Resolution

Here are Some Definitions of a Few of The Terms in the Preceding Slide

6

Definition of "Critical Text"

The Critical Greek Text (CT)

This refers to the Greek New Testament Words that differ from the Traditional Received Text (TR) in over 8,000 places that are found either in (1) the Gnostsic Vatican Manuscript (B), or in (2) the Gnostic Sinai manuscript (Aleph), or in the Greek editions produced (3) by Westcott and Hort, (4) by Nestle and Aland, or (5) by the United Bible Societies.

7

Definition of "Contains"

Contains

transitive verb

to have in it; hold, or include

8

Definition of "Doctrine"

Doctrine

noun

something taught as the principles or creed of a religion

9

Establishing Sound "Doctrine"

How Sound Doctrine Is Esablished

Sound Biblical doctrine or teaching is established by the literal, clear verses found throughout the Bible. If these literal, clear verses are altered, a doctrine might be falsely constructed or weakened.

10

Definition of "Error"

Error

noun

a wrong belief; incorrect opinion

11

The Debate Resolution Rephrased

A REPHRASING OF THE ORIGINAL DEBATE RESOLUTION IN THE LIGHT OF THE PRECEDING DEFINITIONS OF ITS MAIN TERMS

12

Introductions

Introducing the BJU Teachers Making False Statements on Doctrine

13

Dr. Mark Minnick Introduced

Who Is Dr. Mark Minnick?

He is a graduate of Bob Jones University (BJU), a member of the BJU Bible Faculty, the Pastor of Mount Calvary Baptist Church in Greenville, South Carolina, and one of the authors of a BJU-backed book, *From the Mind of God to the Mind of God*. On July 4, 1999, Dr. Minnick held a book-launch for that book in his church. I have a tape recording of this meeting. [This tape has been withdrawn from the public by Minnick's church.] Minnick wrote two of the eighteen chapters of this book, Chapters six and ten. The other authors wrote only one chapter each. The book-launch at his church, and the fact that he wrote two chapters in the book indicates his strong influence in it.

He also wrote one of the chapters in the BJU-backed book, *God's Word in Our Hands—The Bible Preserved For Us.*

14

Dr. Sam Schnaiter Introduced

Who Is Dr. Samuel Schnaiter?

He is a graduate of Bob Jones University (BJU), a Professor of New Testament Language and Literature at BJU, and the Chairman of the BJU Ancient Languages Department. He is the co-author with Ron Tagliapietra of the book entitled *Bible Preservation and the Providence of God*. Due to his important connection with Bob Jones University (BJU), knowing of the procedures at BJU, and the fact that BJU has not protested his position nor recalled the book, I conclude that this book gives not only the position of Dr. Schnaiter, but also that of Bob Jones University itself.

15

Sources For Quotations

The Sources For These Quotations

16

3 Sources For Mark Minnick

Three Sources For Mark Minnick

(1) An audio tape of July 4, 1999, in Mark Minnick's church

(2) *From the Mind of God to the Mind of man* A BJU-approved book.

(3) *God's Word In Our Hands—The Bible Preserved For Us* A BJU-approved book.

17

Source #1 For Mark Minnick

The July 4, 1999 Meeting

On July 4, 1999, Dr. Mark Minnick hosted a book-launch meeting in his Mount Calvary Baptist Church, Greenville, SC.

The purpose of this meeting was to announce a new book: *From the Mind of God to the Mind of Man*. All eight writers were present and gave testimonies about the book.

18

Source #2 For Mark Minnick

From the Mind of God to the Mind of Man
(A BJU-Approved Book)

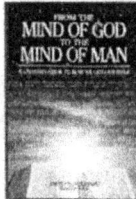

19

Source #2 For Mark Minnick

This book was ANSWERED by the following book

20

Source #2 For Mark Minnick

Fundamentalist Mis-Information On Bible Versions (By Dr. D. A. Waite)

21

Source #3 For Mark Minnick

God's Word In Our Hands
(A BJU-Approved Book)

22

Source #3 For Mark Minnick

This book was ANSWERED by the following book

23

Source #3 For Mark Minnick

Fundamentalist Deception On Bible Versions (By Dr. D. A. Waite)

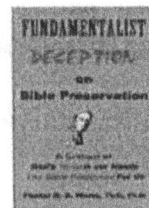

24

The Source For Sam Schnaiter

The Source of the Quotations

For BJU teacher, Dr. Samuel Schnaiter, there is one book from which the quotations were taken:

Bible Preservation and the Providence of God (A BJU-approved book.

25

The Source For Sam Schnaiter

Bible Preservation and the Providence of God
A BJU-Approved Book

26

The Source For Sam Schnaiter

This book was ANSWERED by the following book

27

The Source For Sam Schnaiter

Bob Jones University's Errors On Bible Preservation (By Dr. D. A. Waite)

28

Four Quotes By Mark Minnick

Quotes from Dr. Mark Minnick

29

Source #1 For Mark Minnick

The July 4, 1999 Meeting

On July 4, 1999, Dr. Mark Minnick hosted a book-launch meeting in his Mount Calvary Baptist Church, Greenville, SC.

The purpose of this meeting was to announce a new book: *From the Mind of God to the Mind of Man.* All eight writers were present and gave testimonies about the book.

30

Mark Minnick Quote #1

The subject being discussed concerned the various "*differences*" that occur in the various Greek texts.

Minnick asked the other seven writers of the book: "*Do ANY of those [DIFFERENCES] AFFECT ANY DOCTRINES that we believe?*"

After all seven other authors of the *Mind of Man* book said "*No,*" Dr. Minnick said "*NONE of them do.*"

This is from the audiotape of this meeting. It is found in my book, *Fundamentalist Mis-Information on Bible Versions*, (FM), p. 12.

31

Definitions from Quote #1

Here are Some Definitions of a Few of The Terms in the Preceding Slide

32

Definition of "Any"

Any

adjective

even one

33

Definition of "Difference"

Difference

noun
instance of being different

34

Definition of "Affect"

Affect
(*transitive verb*
to have an effect on; influence;

35

Definition of "Doctrine"

Any

adjective
even one

36

Definition of "Doctrine"

Doctrine

noun

something taught as the principles or creed of a religion

37

Definition of "None"

None

pronoun

1 not one

2 not any

38

Minnick's Quote #1 Rephrased

A REPHRASING OF DR. MINNICK'S QUOTE #1 IN THE LIGHT OF THE PRECEDING DEFINITIONS OF ITS MAIN TERMS

39

The TRUTH About FALSE Doctrine in the W/H Texts

Dr. Jack Moorman has listed 356 PASSAGES in the Greek N.T. Text INVOLVING DOCTRINE (pp. 119-312) where the W/H-type Greek Text differs from the T.R. It is BFT #3230 (456 pages hardback @ $20.00 + $5.00 S&H).

Early Manuscripts, Church Fathers, and the Authorized Version

WITH MANUSCRIPT DIGESTS AND SUMMARIES

J. A. Moorman

40

In Chapter V of
DEFENDING
THE KING JAMES BIBLE
(BFT #1594 @ $12.00
+ $5.00 S&H)
I have listed 168
of these 356 passages
that are doctrinal
errors found in the
Critical Greek Texts

DEFENDING
THE
KING JAMES
BIBLE

A fourfold superiority:

- Texts
- Translators
- Technique
- Theology

God's Word Kept Intact in English

Pastor D. A. Waite, Th.D., Ph.D.
President, The Bible For Today, Inc.

Abbreviations of Translations

KJB–King James Bible
    (All verses used are from the KJB)
NASV–New American Standard Version
NIV–New International Version
ESV–English Standard Version
HCSB–Holman Christian Study Bible
NKJV-FN–New King James Version
    (Footnotes–Study Edition Only)
NB–New Berkley Version
Many Other Versions Could Be Cited

42

Minnick Quote #1 Refuted

1 John 5:7-8–The Denial of the Trinity.

"For there are three that bear record *in heaven, the Father, the Word, and the Holy Ghost: and these three are one.*" (1 John 5:7) "*And there are three that bear witness in earth*, the spirit, and the water, and the blood: and these three agree in one." (1 John 5:7-8)

Greek Texts: -B/ALEPH;

English Versions: (-6) -NIV, -NASV, -NKJV-FN, -NB, -ESV, -HCSB

43

Minnick Quote #1 Refuted

John 3:15--The Denial of the Reality of Perishing in Hell.

"That whosoer believeth in Him *should not perish*, but have eternal life." (John 3:15)

Greek Texts: -B/ALEPH

English Versions: (-5) -NIV, -NASV, -NKJV-FN, -ESV, -HCSB

44

#2 Source For Mark Minnick

From the Mind of God
to the Mind of Man
(A BJU-Approved Book)

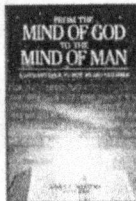

45

Source #2 For Mark Minnick

Fundamentalist Mis-Information On Bible Versions (By Dr. D. A. Waite)

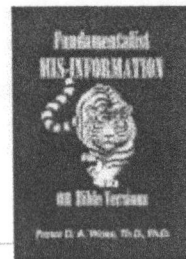

46

Mark Minnick Quote #2

78. MIS-INFORMATION Issue #78. This is from *The Mind of Man*, p. 97. Dr. Minnick wrote:

"So why are writers and preachers today preoccupying and even dividing the Lord's people with the compli-cated and **RELATIVELY INCONSE-QUENTIAL DIFFERENCES** between manuscript families?" [From my book (FM), p. 78]

47

Definitions From Quote #2

Here are Some Definitions of a Few of The Terms in the Preceding Slide

48

Definition of "Relatively"

Relatively

adverb

in a relative manner;

49

Definition of "Inconsequential"

Inconsequential

adjective

of no consequence; unim-portant; trivial

50

Definition of "Difference"

Difference

noun

instance of being different

51

Minnick's Quote #2 Rephrased

A REPHRASING OF DR. MINNICK'S QUOTE #2 IN THE LIGHT OF THE PRECEDING DEFINITIONS OF ITS MAIN TERMS

52

Minnick Quote #2 Refuted

2 Peter 2:17--Denying Eternal Hell

"These are wells without water, clouds that are carried with a tempest; to whom the mist of darkness is reserved *for ever*." (2 Peter 2:17)

Greek Texts: -B/ALEPH

English Versions: (-6) -NIV, -NASV, NKJV-FN, -NB, -ESV, -HCSB

53

Minnick Quote #2 Refuted

1 Peter 2:2--The Denial That Salvation Is by Faith Rather Than by "Growth."

"As newborn babes, desire the sincere milk of the word, that ye may *grow thereby*." (1 Peter 2:2)

Greek Texts: -B/ALEPH

English Versions: (-6) -NIV, -NASV, -NKJV-FN, -NB, -ESV, -HCSB

54

#3 Source For Mark Minnick

God's Word In Our Hands
(A BJU-Approved Book)

55

Source #3 For Mark Minnick

Fundamentalist Deception On Bible Versions (By Dr. D. A. Waite)

56

Mark Minnick Quote #3

From Minnick's Chapter XI: "How Much Difference Do the Differences Make?"

Quotation #198. [From *God's Word in Our Hands* (GWIH), p. 229] Speaking of those standing for the TR and KJB, Minnick wrote: "They ALLEGE that [1] the old manuscripts behind the MODERN GREEK TEXT were ALTERED by HERETICS. [2] The Modern Greek text is a much different New Testament than the Textus Receptus. [3] Every modern version based on the MODERN GREEK TEXT UNDERMINES MAJOR DOCTRINES." [From my book (FD) p. 83] 57

Definitions From Quote #3

Here are Some Definitions of a Few of The Terms in the First Part of the Preceding Slide

58

The "Modern Greek Text"

The Modern Greek Text

The "Modern Greek Text" refers to the over 8,000 Greek New Testament words (that differ from the Traditional Received Text) that are found in the Greek editions produced by (1) Westcott and Hort, (2) Nestle and Aland, or (3) the United Bible Societies.

59

Definition of "Alter"

Alter
intransitive verb
   to become different; change;

60

Definition of "Heretics"

Heretics (Like Gnostics)

noun

an occult salvational system

61

Minnick's Quote #3 Rephrased

A REPHRASING OF DR. MINNICK'S QUOTE #3 IN THE LIGHT OF THE PRECEDING DEFINITIONS OF ITS MAIN TERMS

62

The Fact of Gnostic Influences

There Were Influences By Gnosticism On Bible Versions

Find Out More About This From Pastor D. A. Waite, Th.D., Ph.D. 900 Park Avenue, Collingswood, NJ 08108 856-854-4747; BFT@BibleForToday.org

63

The Source of Gnostic Quotes

All of the following Gnostic quotations here are from the book: *GNOSTICISM: The Doctrinal Foundation of the New Bible Versions* By Mrs. Janet Moser.

It is BFT #2732, 235 large pages @ $25.00 + S&P)

64

Headquarters of Gnosticism

According to the Gnostics, "The Place and headquarters of the true church and God's temple is in Alexandria, Egypt" (p. 212)

65

Origin of Gnostic Greek Texts

Alexandria, Egypt, was the headquarters of the Gnostic doctrinal heresies. The Vatican and Sinai Greek Manuscripts were also from Alexandria. Most modern Bibles in all languages are based upon these manuscripts. They are filled with Gnostic heresies.

66

18 Gnostic Errors in Modern Versions

1. Gnostics separate "Christ" from "Jesus." (GNOSTICISM, p.27)
2. Gnostics deny the Deity of Jesus Christ as "Lord." (GNOSTICISM, p.27)
3. Gnostics deny the Lord Jesus Christ is the Son of God. (GNOSTICISM, p.27)
4. Gnostics deny the Lord Jesus Christ's special relation to His Father. (GNOSTICISM, p.27)
5. Gnostics deny the Lord Jesus Christ's bodily resurrection & ability to raise the dead. (GNOSTICISM, p.27)
6. Gnostics deny the truth about the blood of the Lord Jesus Christ. (GNOSTICISM, p.27)

18 Gnostic Errors in Modern Versions

7. Gnostics believe everyone will be saved. (GNOSTICISM, p.182)
8. Gnostics deny the need of salvation. (GNOSTICISM, p.182)
9. Gnostics deny the need to believe on the Lord Jesus Christ. (GNOSTICISM, p.182)
10. Gnostics deny the virgin birth of the the Lord Jesus Christ. (GNOSTICISM, p.27)
11. Gnostics deny the sinlessness and truthfulness of the Lord Jesus Christ. (GNOSTICISM, p.27)
12. Gnostics deny that the Lord Jesus Christ was the Creator. (GNOSTICISM, p.27)

68

18 Gnostic Errors in Modern Versions

13. Gnostics deny the Trinity. (GNOSTICISM, p.27)
14. Gnostics deny the Omnipresence of the Lord Jesus Christ. (GNOSTICISM, p.27)
15. Gnostics deny that "God" was manifest in the flesh (the Incarnation.) GNOSTICISM, p.27)
16. Gnostics deny the mission of Jesus Christ. (GNOSTICISM, p.27)
17. Gnostics deny the Omnipotence of the Lord Jesus Christ. (GNOSTICISM, p.27)
18. Gnostics deny that the Lord Jesus Christ can give strength. (GNOSTICISM, p.27)

69

Mark Minnick Quote #3

From Minnick's Chapter XI: "How Much Difference Do the Differences Make?"

Quotation #198. [From *God's Word in Our Hands* (GWIH), p. 229] Speaking of those standing for the TR and KJB, Minnick wrote: "They allege that [1] the old manuscripts behind the MODERN GREEK TEXT were ALTERED by HERETICS. [2] The Modern Greek text is a much different New Testament than the Textus Receptus. [3] Every modern version based on the MODERN GREEK TEXT UNDERMINES MAJOR DOCTRINES." [From my book (FD) p. 83]

Mark Minnick Quote #3

Let Me Digress From the Main Subject For A Few Moments

Minnick wrote: "They (the KJB and TR people) ALLEGE that . . . [2] The Modern Greek text is a much different New Testament than the Textus Receptus." [GWIH, p. 83]

Though Minnick denies this, look at the next slide.

71

8,000 CT/TR Differences

"8,000 Differences Between the Textus Receptus and the Nestle & Aland and NT Greek Texts" (BFT #3084) 544 pages ($20.00 + $5.00 S&H) Hardback Book By Dr. Jack Moorman. A careful research document.

72

Definitions From Quote #3

Here are Some Definitions of a Few of the Terms in the Last Part of the Preceding Slide

73

The "Modern Greek Text"

The Modern Greek Text

The "Modern Greek Text" refers to the over 8,000 Greek New Testament words (that differ from the Traditional Received Text) that are found in the Greek editions produced by (1) Westcott and Hort, (2) Nestle and Aland, or (3) the United Bible Societies.

74

Definition of "Undermine"

Undermine

transitive verb

to wear away and weaken the supports of; esp. by subtle, stealthy, or insidious means

75

Definition of "Major"

Major

adjective

greater in importance or rank

76

Definition of "Doctrine"

Doctrine

noun

something taught as the principles or creed of a religion

77

Minnick's Quote #3 Rephrased

A REPHRASING OF DR. MINNICK'S QUOTE #3 IN THE LIGHT OF THE PRECEDING DEFINITIONS OF ITS MAIN TERMS

78

Minnick Quote #3 Refuted

Romans 5:1--The Denial of Instantaneous Peace with God.

"Therefore being justified by faith, *we have* peace with God through our Lord Jesus Christ:" (Romans 5:1)

Greek Texts: -B/ALEPH

English Versions: (-2) -NKJV-FN, -NB

79

Minnick Quote #3 Refuted

1 Corinthians 5:7--The Denial of Christ's Substitutionary, Vicarious Atonement.

(1) 1 Corinthians 5:7.

"Purge out therefore the old leaven, that ye may be a new lump, as ye are un-leavened. For even Christ our passover is sacrificed *for us*:" (1 Corinthians 5:7)

Greek Texts: -B/ALEPH

English Versions: (-6) -NIV, -NASV, -NKJV-FN, -NB ,-ESV, -HCSB

80

Mark Minnick Quote #4

Quotation #221. (From GWIH, p. 271) "<u>NOT</u> a <u>SINGLE</u> <u>VARIANT</u> in <u>ANY</u> way <u>ALTERS</u> what Christians <u>BELIEVE</u> and <u>PRACTICE</u>. Every <u>VARIANT</u> could be <u>IN-CLUDEED</u> in our Bibles or <u>EVERY ONE</u> could be <u>OMITTED</u> and it would not <u>AFFECT</u> our FAITH or <u>PRACTICE</u> in the <u>SLIGHTEST</u> way." [From my book (FD) p. 90]

81

Definitions From Quote #4

Here are Some Definitions of a Few of The Terms in the Preceding Slide

82

Definition of "Not"

Not

adverb
  <u>to no degree;</u>

83

Definition of "Single"

Single

adjective
  <u>one only</u>

84

Definition of "Variant"

Variant

noun

anything that is variant, as a different spelling of the same word,

85

Definition of "Any"

Any

adjective

even one;

86

Definition of "Alter"

Alter

intransitive verb

to become different; change;

87

Definition of "Believe"

Believe

transitive verb

to take as true

88

Definition of "Practice"

Practice

noun

a frequent or usual action; habit; usage

89

Definition of "Variant"

Variant

noun

anything that is variant, as a different spelling of the same word

90

Definition of "Included"

Included

adjective

enclosed, contained

91

Definition of "Every"

Every

adjective

each

92

Definition of "Omit"

Omit

transitive verb

to fail to include; leave out

93

Definition of "Affect"

Affect

(*transitive verb*

to have an effect on; influence;

94

Definition of "Faith"

Faith

noun

a system of religious beliefs

95

Definition of "Slight"

Slight

adjective

having little weight, small in amount

96

Minnick's Quote #4 Rephrased

A REPHRASING OF DR. MINNICK'S QUOTE #4 IN THE LIGHT OF THE PRECEDING DEFINITIONS OF ITS MAIN TERMS

97

Minnick Quote #4 Refuted

1 Peter 4:1--Denying Christ's Substitutionary, Vicarious Atonement

"Forasmuch then as Christ hath suffered _for us_ in the flesh, arm yourselves like-wise with the same mind: for He that hath suffered in the flesh hath ceased from sin;"   (1 Peter 4:1)

Greek Texts: -B

English Versions: (-6): -NIV, -NASV, -NKJV-FN, -NB ,-ESV, -HCSB

98

Minnick Quote #4 Refuted

Colossians 1:14--Christ's Blood Removed

"In whom we have redemption _through His blood_, {even} the for-giveness of sins:"   (Colossians 1:14)

Greek Texts: -B/ALEPH

English Versions: (-5) -NIV, -NASV, -NKJV-FN, -ESV, -HCSB

99

13 Quotes by Sam Schnaiter

Quotes From Dr. Sam Schnaiter

100

Source For Sam Schnaiter

Bible Preservation and the Providence of God
A BJU-Approved Book

101

Source For Sam Schnaiter

Bob Jones University's Errors On Bible Preservation (By Dr. D. A. Waite)

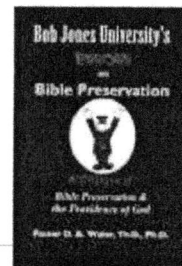

102

Sam Schnaiter Quote #1

STATEMENT #85: (From BP, p. 83) "NONE of these [MS] VARIANTS AFFECT meaning much less DOCTRINE." [From my book (BJUE), p. 37]

103

Definitions From Quote #1

Here are Some Definitions of a Few of The Terms in the Preceding Slide

104

Definition of "None"

None

pronoun

not one; not any

105

Definition of "Variant"

Variant

noun

anything that is variant, as a different spelling of the same word

106

Definition of "Affect"

Affect

(*transitive verb*

to have an effect on; influence;

107

Definition of "Doctrine"

Doctrine

noun

something taught as the principles or creed of a religion

108

Schnaiter's Quote #1 Rephrased

A REPHRASING OF DR. SCHNAITER'S QUOTE #1 IN THE LIGHT OF THE PRECEDING DEFINITIONS OF ITS MAIN TERMS

109

Schnaiter Quote #1 Refuted

John 6:47--Christ Is Not Necessary for Everlasitng Life

"Verily, verily, I say unto you, He that believeth *on Me* hath everlasting life." (John 6:47)

Greek Texts: -B/ALEPH

English Versions: (-5) -NIV, -NASV, -NKJV-FN, -ESV, -HCSB

110

Schnaiter Quote #1 Refuted

Romans 1:16—"Christ" Is Removed from The Gospel

"For I am not ashamed of the gospel *of Christ*: for it is the power of God unto salvation to every one that believeth; to the Jew first, and also to the Greek." (Romans 1:16)

Greek Texts: -B/ALEPH

English Versions: (-6) -NIV, -NASV, -NKJV-FN, -NB, ESV, -HCSB

111

Sam Schnaiter Quote #2

STATEMENT #87: (From BP, p. 84) "The most **IMPORTANT CONCLUSION** is that even those **FEW VARIANTS** that affect meaning do **NOT AFFECT DOCTRINE.**" [From my book (BJUE), p. 38]

112

Definitions From Quote #2

Here are Some Definitions of a Few of The Terms in the Preceding Slide

113

Definition of "Important"

Important

adjective

having much significance

114

Definition of "Conclusion"

Conclusion

noun

the last step in a reasoning process;

115

Definition of "Few"

Few

adjective

not many; a small number of

116

Definition of "Variant"

Variant

noun

anything that is variant, as a different spelling of the same word

117

Definition of "Not"

Not

adverb

in no manner; to no degree

118

Definition of "Affect"

Affect

(*transitive verb*

to have an effect on; influence

119

Definition of "Doctrine"

Doctrine

noun

something taught as the principles or creed of a religion,

120

Schnaiter's Quote #2 Rephrased

A REPHRASING OF DR. SCHNAITER'S QUOTE #2 IN THE LIGHT OF THE PRECEDING DEFINITIONS OF ITS MAIN TERMS

121

Schnaiter Quote #2 Refuted

Galatians 4:7--An "Heir" of God Without Christ

"Wherefore thou art no more a servant, but a son; and if a son, then an heir of God *through Christ*." (Galatians 4:7)

Greek Texts: -B/ALEPH

English Versions: (-6) -NIV, -NASV, -NKJV-FN, -NB, -ESV, -HCSB

122

Schnaiter Quote #2 Refuted

Hebrews 1:3--Christ Purged Sins All "By Himself" Was Removed

"Who being the brightness of {His} glory, and the express image of His person, and upholding all things by the word of His power, when He had *by Himself* purged our sins, sat down on the right hand of the Majesty on high;" (Hebrews 1:3)

Greek Texts: -B/ALEPH

English Versions: (-6) -NIV, -NASV, -NKJV-FN, -NB, -ESV, -HCSB

123

Sam Schnaiter Quote #3

STATEMENT #88: (From BP, p. 84) "It cannot be stressed too heavily that not one TEXTUAL VARIANT AFFECTS even ONE SINGLE TEACHING of SCRIPTURE. Fully 100% of the GREEK NEW TESTAMENT is FREE from VARIANTS that ALTER DOCTRINE." [From my book (BJUE), p. 38]

124

Definitions From Quote #3

Here are Some Definitions of a Few of The Terms in the Preceding Slide

125

Definition of "Textual"

Textual

adjective

conforming to a text

126

Definition of "Variant"

Variant

noun

anything that is variant, as a different spelling of the same word

127

Definition of "Affect"

Affect

(*transitive verb*

to have an effect on; influence

128

Definition of "One"

One

adjective

a single thing or unit;

129

Definition of "Single"

Single

adjective

one only; one and no more;

130

Definition of "Teaching"

Teaching

noun

something taught; doctrine, or instruction

131

Definition of "Scripture"

Scripture

noun

the Christian Bible; Old and New Testaments

132

Definition of "100%"

100%

This is 100 out of 100; complete.

133

Definition of "Greek NT"

The Greek New Testament

This includes the Greek New Testament Words that differ from the Traditional Received Text (TR) in over 8,000 places that are found either in the (1) Vatican Manuscript (B), (2) Sinai manuscript (Aleph), Greek editions produced by (3) Westcott and Hort, (4) Nestle and Aland, or (5) the United Bible Societies.

134

Definition of "Free"

Free

adjective

independent

135

Definition of "Variant"

Variant

noun

anything that is variant, as a different spelling of the same word

136

Definition of "Alter"

Alter

transitive verb

to make different in details; modify

137

Definition of "Doctrine"

Doctrine

noun

something taught as the principles or creed of a religion

138

Schnaiter's Quote #3 Rephrased

A REPHRASING OF DR. SCHNAITER'S QUOTE #3 IN THE LIGHT OF THE PRECEDING DEFINITIONS OF ITS MAIN TERMS

139

Schnaiter Quote #3 Refuted

John 3:13--The Denial of the Omnipresence of Christ.

"And no man hath ascended up to heaven, but He that came down from heaven, {even} the Son of man *Which is in heaven*." (John 3:13)

Greek Texts: -B/ALEPH

English Versions: (-5) -NIV, -NASV, -NKJV-FN, -ESV, -HCSB

140

Schnaiter Quote #3 Refuted

1 Timothy 3:16—The Denial That Christ Was "God" Manifest in The Flesh.

"And without controversy great is the mystery of godliness: *God* was manifest in the flesh, justified in the Spirit, seen of angels, preached unto the Gentiles, believed on in the world, received up into glory." (1 Timothy 3:16)

Greek Texts: -ALEPH (No B in 1 Timothy)

English Versions: (-6) -NIV, -NASV, -NKJV-FN, -NB, -ESV, -HCSB

141

Sam Schnaiter Quote #4

STATEMENT   #108: (From BP, p. 96) Quoting with approval: ". . . Bengel proved that **MANUSCRIPT VARIATION** does **NOT AFFECT DOCTRINE**, and his theories earned him the title Father of Textual Criticism." [From my book (BJUE), p. 46]

142

Definitions From Quote #4

Here are Some Definitions of a Few of The Terms in the Preceding Slide

143

Definition of "Manuscript"

Manuscript

noun

a book or document written by hand

144

Definition of "Variation"

Variation

noun

change or deviation in form, condition, appearance, extent, etc. from a former or usual state, or from an assumed standard

145

Definition of "Not"

Not

adverb

in no manner; to no degree

146

Definition of "Affect"

Affect

(*transitive verb*

to have an effect on; influence

147

Definition of "Doctrine"

Doctrine

noun

something taught as the principles or creed of a religion

148

Schnaiter's Quote #4 Rephrased

A REPHRASING OF DR. SCHNAITER'S QUOTE #4 IN THE LIGHT OF THE PRECEDING DEFINITIONS OF ITS MAIN TERMS

149

Schnaiter Quote #4 Refuted

1 John 4:3--The Denial that the Lord Jesus Christ as "come in the flesh"

"And every spirit that confesseth not that Jesus *Christ is come in the flesh* is not of God: and this is that {spirit} of antichrist, whereof ye have heard that it should come; and even now already is it in the world." (1 John 4:3)

Greek Texts: -B (No ALEPH here)

English Versions: (-4) -NASV, -NKJV-FN, -ESV, -HCSB

150

Schnaiter Quote #4 Refuted

Luke 2:22--The Denial of the Sinlessness of the Lord Jesus Christ.

"And when the days of *her* purification according to the law of Moses were accomplished, they brought him to Jerusalem, to present {him} to the Lord;" (Luke 2:22)

Greek Texts: -B/ALEPH

English Versions: (-5) -NIV, -NASV, -NB, -ESV, -HCSB

151

Sam Schnaiter Quote #5

STATEMENT #111: (From BP, p. 97) He cites six men and then says: ". . . they [the manuscripts] disagree on the manner and details. All of them agree that **NOT** a **SINGLE DOCTRINE** of **SCRIPTURE** is in **QUESTION**." [From my book (BJUE), p. 47]

152

Definitions From Quote #5

Here are Some Definitions of a Few of The Terms in the Preceding Slide

153

Definition of "Not"

Not

adverb
   in no manner; to no degree

154

Definition of "Single"

Single

adjective
   one only; one and no more

155

Definition of "Doctrine"

Doctrine

noun
   something taught as the principles or creed of a religion

156

Definition of "Scripture"

Scripture

noun

the Christian Bible; Old and New Testaments

157

Definition of "Question"

Question

noun

doubt; uncertainty

158

Schnaiter's Quote #5 Rephrased

A REPHRASING OF DR. SCHNAITER'S QUOTE #5 IN THE LIGHT OF THE PRECEDING DEFINITIONS OF ITS MAIN TERMS

159

Schnaiter Quote #5 Refuted

Matthew 18:11--The Denial of the Mission of the Lord Jesus Christ.

"*For the Son of man is come to save that which was lost.*" (Matthew 18:11)

Greek Texts: -B/ALEPH

English Versions: (-4) -NIV, -ASV, -NKJV-FN, -ESV

160

Schnaiter Quote #5 Refuted

Luke 9:56--The Denial of the Mission of the Lord Jesus Christ.

"*For the Son of man is not come to destroy men's lives, but to save {them}.* And they went to another village." (Luke 9:56)

Greek Texts: -B/ALEPH

English Versions: (-5) -NIV, -NASV, -NKJV-FN,-ESV, -HCSB

161

Sam Schnaiter Quote #6

STATEMENT #115: (From PB, p. 103) "Third, and most important, __NONE__ of these views [on "*textual variants*"] necessarily __DISTURBS__ the __ORTHODOXY__ of the __CHRISTIAN__ Church as __PLAINLY TAUGHT__ in the __SCRIPTURES__." [From my book (BJUE), p. 48]

162

Definitions From Quote #6

Here are Some Definitions of a Few of The Terms in the Preceding Slide

163

Definition of "None"

None

pronoun

not one

164

Definition of "Disturb"

Disturb

transitive verb

to break up the settled order or orderly working of

165

Definition of "Orthodoxy"

Orthodoxy

adjective

conforming to the Christian faith as formulated in the early ecumenical creeds and con-fessions

166

Definition of "Christian"

Christian

Adjective

of or representing Christians or Christianity

167

Definition of "Plain"

Plain

adjective

clearly understood; evident; obvious

168

Definition of "Taught"

Teach

transitive verb

<u>to show or help to learn</u>

169

Definition of "Scripture"

Scripture

noun

<u>the Christian Bible; Old and New Testaments</u>

170

Schnaiter's Quote #6 Rephrased

A REPHRASING OF DR. SCHNAITER'S QUOTE #6 IN THE LIGHT OF THE PRECEDING DEFINITIONS OF ITS MAIN TERMS

171

Schnaiter Quote #6 Refuted

Matthew 1:25--The Denial of the Virgin Birth of the Lord Jesus Christ.

"And knew her not till she had brought forth her *Firstborn* Son: and he called His name JESUS." (Matthew 1:25)

Greek Texts: -B/ALEPH

English Versions: (-5) -NIV, -NASV, -NKJV-FN, -ESV, -HCSB

172

Schnaiter Quote #6 Refuted

Luke 2:33--The Denial of the Virgin Birth of the Lord Jesus Christ

"And *Joseph* and his mother marvelled at those things which were spoken of him." (Luke 2:33)

Greek Texts: -B/ALEPH

English Versions: (-6) -NIV, -NASV, -NKJV-FN, -NB, -ESV, -HCSB

173

Sam Schnaiter Quote #7

STATEMENT #131: (From PB, p. 120) "The <u>VARIANTS</u> have minimal importance to preservation because they are comparatively <u>FEW</u>, and because <u>NO CHRISTIAN DOCTRINE</u> is <u>AFFECTED</u> by them." [From my book (BJUE), p. 55]

174

Definitions From Quote #7

Here are Some Definitions of a Few of The Terms in the Preceding Slide

175

Definition of "Variant"

Variant

noun

anything that is variant, as a different spelling of the same word.

176

Definition of "Few"

Few

adjective

not many; a small number

177

Definition of "No"

No

adverb

not in any degree; not at all

178

Definition of "Christian"

Christian

Adjective

of Jesus Christ or his teach-ings

179

Definition of "Doctrine"

Doctrine

noun

something taught as the prin-ciples or creed of a religion

180

Definition of "Affect"

Affect

(*transitive verb*

to have an effect on; influence

181

Schnaiter's Quote #7 Rephrased

**A REPHRASING OF DR.
SCHNAITER'S QUOTE #7 IN
THE LIGHT OF THE
PRECEDING DEFINITIONS OF
ITS MAIN TERMS**

182

Schnaiter Quote #7 Refuted

**Acts 2:30–The Denial of the Lord Jesus
Christ's Bodily Resurrection**

"Therefore being a prophet, and knowing
that God had sworn with an oath to him,
that of the fruit of his loins, *according to
the flesh, He would raise up Christ* to sit on
his throne;" (Acts 2:30)

Greek Texts: -B/ALEPH

**English Versions: (-5) -NIV, -NASV, -NKJV-FN,
ESV, -HCSB**

183

Schnaiter Quote #7 Refuted

**John 8:59--Denial of the Omnipotence of
the Lord Jesus Christ**

"Then took they up stones to cast at
Him: but Jesus hid Himself, and went
out of the temple, *going through the
midst of them, and so passed by*."
(John 8:59)

Greek Texts: -B/ALEPH

**English Versions: (-6) -NIV, -NASV,
-NKJV-FN, -NB, -ESV, -HCSB**

184

Sam Schnaiter Quote #8

STATEMENT #162: (From PB,
p. 163) [quoting Philip Mauro
with approval] "In other words
the very <u>WORST</u> <u>TEXT</u> that could
be <u>CONSTRUCTED</u> from the
abundant <u>MATERIALS</u> available
would <u>NOT</u> <u>DISTURB</u> <u>ANY</u> of the
<u>GREAT</u> <u>TRUTHS</u> of the <u>CHRI-
TIAN FAITH</u>." [My book (BJU),
[My book (BJUE), p. 68]

185

Definitions From Quote #8

**Here are Some
Definitions of a Few of
The Terms in the
Preceding Slide**

186

Definition of "Worst"

Worst

adjective

of the lowest quality or condition; the least favorable condition

187

Definition of "Text"

Text

noun

the actual structure of words in a piece of writing

188

Definition of "Constructed"

Construct

transitive verb

to build

189

Definition of "Materials"

Material

noun

what a thing is made of

190

Definition of "Not"

Not

adverb

in no manner

191

Definition of "Disturb"

Disturb

transitive verb

to break up the settled order or orderly working of

192

Definition of "Any"

Any

adjective

one, no matter which, of more than two

193

Definition of "Great"

Great

adjective

of most importance

194

Definition of "Truth"

Truth

noun

that which is true; that accords with fact or reality

195

Definition of "Christian"

Christian

adjective

of Jesus Christ or his teachings

196

Definition of "Faith"

Faith

noun

religion or a system of religious beliefs

197

Schnaiter's Quote #8 Rephrased

A REPHRASING OF DR. SCHNAITER'S QUOTE #8 IN THE LIGHT OF THE PRECEDING DEFINITIONS OF ITS MAIN TERMS

198

Schnaiter Quote #8 Refuted

Philippians 4:13--Denial that the Lord Jesus Christ Can Strengthen

"I can do all things through *Christ* Which strengtheneth me." (Philippians 4:13)

Greek Texts: -B/ALEPH

English Versions: (-6) -NIV, -NASV, -NKJV-FN, -NB, -ESV, -HCSB

199

Schnaiter Quote #8 Refuted

2 Corinthians 4:14--The Denial of Christ's Power to Raise the Dead.

"Knowing that He which raised up the Lord Jesus shall raise up us also *by* Jesus, and shall present {us} with you." (2 Corinthians 4:14)

Greek Texts: -B/ALEPH

English Versions: (-6) -NIV, -NASV, -NKJV-FN, -NB, ESV, -HCSB

200

Sam Schnaiter Quote #9

STATEMENT #163: (From PB, p. 163) "If the most liberal of the critical eclectic scholars set out to begin an anti-KJV conspiracy group and <u>CONSISTENTLY</u> <u>CHOSE</u> the <u>WORST</u> possible <u>READINGS</u> from his <u>ALTERNATIVES, NO DOC-TRINAL</u> <u>CHANGES</u> would <u>RE-SULT</u>." [From my book (BJUE), p. 69]

201

Definitions From Quote #9

Here are Some Definitions of a Few of The Terms in the Preceding Slide

202

Definition of "Consistently"

Consistent

adjective

<u>holding always to the same principles or practice</u>

203

Definition of "Chose"

Choose

transitive verb

<u>to pick out by preference from what is available</u>

204

Definition of "Worst"

Worst

adjective

the least favorable condition

205

Definition of "Readings"

Reading

noun

the form of a specified word, sentence, or passage

206

Definition of "Alternatives"

Alternative

noun

a choice between two or among more than two things

207

Definition of "No"

No

adverb

not in any degree

208

Definition of Doctrine

Doctrine

noun

something taught as the principles or creed of a religion

209

Definition of "Changes"

Change

noun

the act or process of substitution, alteration, or variation

210

Definition of "Result"

Result

noun

anything that comes about as a consequence of some action

211

Schnaiter's Quote #9 Rephrased

A REPHRASING OF DR. SCHNAITER'S QUOTE #9 IN THE LIGHT OF THE PRECEDING DEFINITIONS OF ITS MAIN TERMS

212

Schnaiter Quote #9 Refuted

Ephesians 3:9--The Denial of Christ's Power to Create All Things.

"And to make all {men} see what {is} the fellowship of the mystery, which from the beginning of the world hath been hid in God, who created all things *by Jesus Christ*." (Ephesians 3:9)

Greek Texts: -B/ALEPH

English Versions: (-6) -NIV, -NASV, -NKJV-FN, -NB, -ESV, -HCSB

213

Schnaiter Quote #9 Refuted

Luke 23:42--The Denial of Christ's Deity by Removing "Lord"

"And he said unto Jesus, *Lord*, remember me when thou comest into Thy kingdom." (Luke 23:42)

Greek Texts: -B/ALEPH

English Versions: (-6) -NIV, -NASV, -NKJV-FN, -NB,-ESV, -HCSB

214

Sam Schnaiter Quote #10

STATEMENT #179: (From PB, p. 247) "In spite of all the uproar, our first five chapters stressed that these [textual] DIFFERENCES AFFECT very FEW PASSAGES, and NEVER AFFECT DOCTRINE." [From my book (BJUE), p. 76]

215

Definitions From Quote #10

Here are Some Definitions of a Few of The Terms in the Preceding Slide

216

Definition of "Difference"

Difference

noun

condition or instance of be-ing different

217

Definition of "Affect"

Affect

(*transitive verb*

to have an effect on; influ-ence

218

Definition of "Few"

Few

adjective

not many; a small number

219

Definition of "Passage"

Passage

noun

a short segment of a written work [like a Bible *passage*]

220

Definition of "Never"

Never

adverb

not ever; at no time

221

Definition of "Affect"

Affect

(*transitive verb*

to have an effect on; influ-ence

222

Definition of "Doctrine"

Doctrine

noun

<u>something taught as the principles or creed of a religion</u>

223

Schnaiter's Quote #10 Rephrased

A REPHRASING OF DR. SCHNAITER'S QUOTE #10 IN THE LIGHT OF THE PRECEDING DEFINITIONS OF ITS MAIN TERMS

224

Schnaiter Quote #10 Refuted

Romans 6:11--The Denial of Christ's Deity by Removing "Lord"

"Likewise reckon ye also yourselves to be dead indeed unto sin, but alive unto God through Jesus Christ *our Lord*." (Romans 6:11)

Greek Texts: -B

English Versions: (-5) -NIV, -NASV, -NB,-ESV, -HCSB

225

Schnaiter Quote #10 Refuted

1 Corinthians 15:47--The Denial of Christ's Deity by Removing "Lord"

"The first man {is} of the earth, earthy: the second man {is} *the Lord* from heaven." (1 Corinthians 15:47)

Greek Texts: -B/ALEPH

English Versions: (-6) -NIV, -NASV, -NKJV-FN, -NB, -ESV, -HCSB

226

Sam Schnaiter Quote #11

STATEMENT #188: (From PB, p. 263) "We have already shown that <u>NO DOCTRINAL VARIATIONS ARISE REGARD-LESS</u> of <u>WHICH</u> MANUSCRIPTS are <u>USED</u>." [From my book (BJUE), p. 80]

227

Definitions From Quote #11

Here are Some Definitions of a Few of The Terms in the Preceding Slide

228

Definition of "No"

No

adverb

not in any degree; not at all

229

Definition of "Doctrine"

Doctrine

noun

something taught as the principles or creed of a religion

230

Definition of "Variation"

Variation

noun

the act or process of varying

231

Definition of "Arise"

Arise

intransitive verb

to result or spring (*from*)

232

Definition of "Regardless"

Regardless

adjective

without regard

233

Definition of "Which"

Which

adjective

what one or ones (of the number mentioned)

234

Definition of "Manuscripts"

Manuscript

noun

<u>a book or document written by hand</u>

235

Definition of "Use"

Use

transitive verb

<u>employ for a given purpose</u>

236

Schnaiter's Quote #11 Rephrased

A REPHRASING OF DR. SCHNAITER'S QUOTE #11 IN THE LIGHT OF THE PRECEDING DEFINITIONS OF ITS MAIN TERMS

237

Schnaiter Quote #11 Refuted

John 6:69--The Denial that Christ is the Son of God

"And we believe and are sure that Thou art that *Christ, the Son of the living God*." (John 6:69)

Greek Texts: -B/ALEPH

English Versions: (-6) -NIV, -NASV, -NKJV-FN, -NB, -ESV, -HCSB

238

Schnaiter Quote #11 Refuted

Acts 8:37--Denial that the Lord Jesus Christ Is the Son of God

"*And Philip said, If thou believest with all thine heart, thou mayest. And he answered and said, I believe that Jesus Christ is the Son of God.*" (Acts 8:37)

Greek Texts: -B/ALEPH

English Versions: (-4) -NIV, -NASV, -NKJV-FN, -ESV

239

Sam Schnaiter Quote #12

STATEMENT #190: (From PB, p.270) [From Chapter Twelve, "Selecting Versions"] "Most DIF-FERENCES among Bible ver-sions in English are due to issues over how words should be translated rather than which MANUSCRIPTS are the best. This means that a person buying a Bible need NOT get OVERLY CONCERNED about those is-sues." [From my book (BJUE), p. 81]

240

Definitions From Quote #12

Here are Some Definitions of a Few of The Terms in the Preceding Slide

241

Definition of "Difference"

Difference

noun

instance of being different

242

Definition of "Manuscript"

Manuscript

noun

a book or document written by hand

243

Definition of "Not"

Not

adverb

in no manner; to no degree

244

Definition of "Overly"

Overly

adverb

too much; excessively

245

Definition of "Concerned"

Concerned

adjective

uneasy or anxious

246

Definition of "Concerned"

Concerned

adjective

uneasy or anxious

247

Schnaiter's Quote #12 Rephrased

A REPHRASING OF DR. SCHNAITER'S QUOTE #12 IN THE LIGHT OF THE PRECEDING DEFINITIONS OF ITS MAIN TERMS

248

Schnaiter Quote #12 Refuted

John 6:69--Denial that the Lord Jesus Christ Is the Son of God

"And we believe and are sure that Thou art that *Christ, the Son of the living God*." (John 6:69)

Greek Texts: -B/ALEPH

English Versions: (-6) -NIV, -NASV, -NKJV-FN, -NB, -ESV, -HCSB

249

Schnaiter Quote #13 Refuted

The Denial that Jesus Christ Was One Person

One of the heresies of the early church which flourished *especially in the land of* Egypt where manuscripts "B" (Vatican) and "Aleph" (Sinai) originated, was the heresy of "ADOPTIONISM." This heresy taught that there was a distinction between the human "Jesus" and Divine "Christ." This same heresy was carried down through the centuries and appears in Liberalism/Modernism/Apostasy as well as in so-called "Christian Science."

250

Sam Schnaiter Quote #13

STATEMENT #209: (From PB, p. 286) [quoting Richard Bentley with approval] "The real text of sacred writers is competently exact . . . nor is ONE ARTICLE OF FAITH or MORAL PRECEPT either PERVERTED or LOST. . . . Choose as awkwardly as you will, CHOOSE the WORST by DESIGN, out of the WHOLE lump of readings." [From my book (BJUE), p. 95]

251

Definition of "One"

One

adjective

a single thing

252

Definitions From Quote #13

Here are Some Definitions of a Few of The Terms in the Preceding Slide

253

Definition of "One"

One

adjective

<u>a single thing</u>

254

Definition of "Faith"

Faith (Articles of)

noun

<u>a religion or a system of religious beliefs</u>

255

Definition of "Moral"

Moral

adjective

<u>the principles of right and wrong</u>

256

Definition of "Precept"

Precept

noun

<u>a rule of moral conduct</u>

257

Definition of "Perverted"

Perverted

adjective

<u>deviating from what is considered right</u>

258

Definition of "Lost"

Lost

adjective

not to be found; missing

259

Definition of "Choose"

Choose

transitive verb

to pick out by preference from what is available

260

Definition of "Worst"

Worst

adjective

of the lowest quality or con-dition

261

Definition of "Design"

Design

noun

purpose; intention; or aim

262

Definition of "Whole"

Whole

adjective

entire; complete

263

Schnaiter's Quote #13 Rephrased

A REPHRASING OF DR. SCHNAITER'S QUOTE #13 IN THE LIGHT OF THE PRECEDING DEFINITIONS OF ITS MAIN TERMS

264

Schnaiter Quote #13 Refuted

Romans 15:8--The Denial that Jesus Christ Was One Person

"Now I say that *Jesus* Christ was a minister of the circumcision for the truth of God, to confirm the promises {made} unto the fathers:" (Romans 15:8)

Greek Texts: -B/ALEPH

English Versions: (-5) -NIV, -NASV, -NB,-ESV, -HCSB 265

Schnaiter Quote #13 Refuted

2 Corinthians 5:18--The Denial that Jesus Christ Was One Person

"And all things {are} of God, who hath reconciled us to himself by *Jesus* Christ, and hath given to us the ministry of reconciliation;" (2 Corinthians 5:18)

Greek Texts: -B/ALEPH

English Versions: (-5) -NIV, -NASV, -NB, -ESV, -HCSB 266

Various Doctored Doctrines

What CONCLUSIONS Can Be Drawn From The 17 Statements By These Two BJU Teachers? 267

Some Important Definitions

Other Important Definitions 268

Hebrew & Greek Definitions

Hebrew and Greek Definitions 269

Hebrew & Greek Definitions

The Hebrew Word For FALSEHOOD

08267 sheqer {sheh'-ker} (2 Samuel 18:13)
1) lie, deception, disappointment, falsehood
 1a) deception (what deceives or disappoints or betrays one)
 1b) deceit, fraud, wrong 270

Hebrew & Greek Definitions

The Greek Word For FALSE

5571 pseudes 1) lying, <u>deceitful</u>, false

271

Some English Definitions

English Definitions of "Lie" and Some Synonyms

272

Definition of "Lie"

Lie

noun

<u>anything that gives or is meant to give a false impression</u>

273

Definition of "Prevaricate"

Prevaricate

intransitive verb

<u>to turn aside from, or evade, the truth;</u>

274

Definition of "Equivocate"

Equivocate

intransitive verb

<u>to use equivocal terms in order to deceive, mislead,</u>

275

Definition of "Fabricate"

Fabricate

transitive verb

<u>to make up; invent</u>

276

Definition of "Fib"

Fib

noun

a small or trivial lie

277

Definition of "Truth"

**"Sanctify them through thy truth: thy word is truth."
(John 17:17)**

278

Any of the following books are available from:

THE BIBLE FOR TODAY PRESS

900 Park Avenue
Collingswood, New Jersey 08108
U.S.A.

Church Phone: 856-854-4747

BFT Phone: 856-854-4452

Orders: 1-800-John 10:9

email: BFT@BibleForToday.org

Website:www.BibleForToday.org

Fax: 856-854-2464

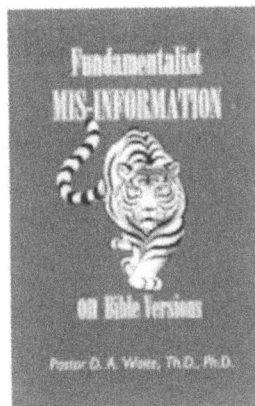

This book, *Fundametalist Mis-Information on Bible Versions* by Dr. D. A. Waite, Th.D., Ph.D. is important because it is an answer to a book published by avowed Fundamentalists with the enthusiastic support of Bob Jones University. That book is called "From the Mind of God to the Mind of Man", written by graduates, faculty members, Trustee Board members, Cooperating Board members, and friends of Bob Jones University. Some of the extensive amount of Mis-Information contained in "The Mind Of Man" has been answered in other books Dr. Waite has written; but, it was coming from Neo-Evangelical and Liberal/Moderistic sources, whereas the present study exposes and refutes Mis-Information from those who call themselves Fundamentalists. B.F.T. #2974 for a gift of $11.00 + $5.00 S&H.

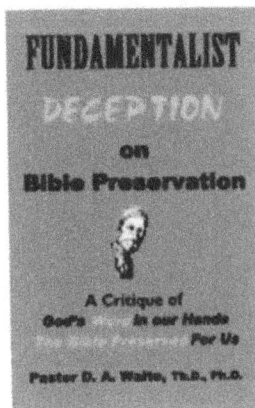

This book, *Fundamentalist Deception on Bible Preservation* by Dr. D. A. Waite, Th.D., Ph.D. is important because it is an answer to a second book published by avowed Fundamentalists with the enthusiastic support of Bob Jones III, then President of Bob Jones University (BJU). Sadly, BJU deception on Bible preservation has had a pervasive influence on Bible institutes, colleges, universities, churches, and individuals both in the US and on many of the mission fields of the world. This book seeks to combate and correct the mis-information promulgated by BJU's influence. B.F.T. #3234 for a gift of $12.00 + $5.00 S&H.

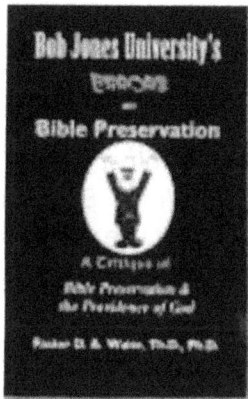

This book, *Bob Jones University's Errors on Bible Preservation* by Dr. D. A. Waite, Th.D., Ph.D. is in response to a book, *Bible Preservation and the Providence of God* by Samuel Schnaiter and Ron Tagliapietra who are associated with Bob Jones University (BJU) . Dr. Waite refutes their deceptions concerning true Bible Preservation. He clear points out that the authors associated with BJU do not believe in preservation of the Words, but rather preservation of "ideas, thoughts, concepts, message, truth, or teachings. This is serious error. Furthermore, the BFU men declare the original words to be "reliable," but not inerrant. Dr. Waite addresses many other statements that are deceptive in his book. BFT #3259 for a gift of $8.00 + $5.00 S&H.

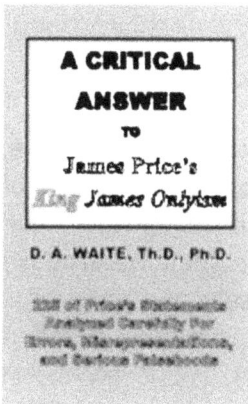

Pastor D. A. Waite, Th.D., Ph.D. has written a succinct and valuable book, *A Critical Answer to James Price's King James Onlyism*, a refutation of James D. Price's recently published book, *King James Onlyism: A New Sect*, explaining his false positions. According to Dr. Waite, Price has propounded a disbelief in the preservation of the original Hebrew, Aramaic, and Greek Words, and he refers to those who maintain the position as "King James Only." Dr. Waite has analyzed 225 of Price's statements and notated errors, misrepresentations, and serious falsehoods. BFT #3375 for a gift of $11.00 + $5.00 S&H.

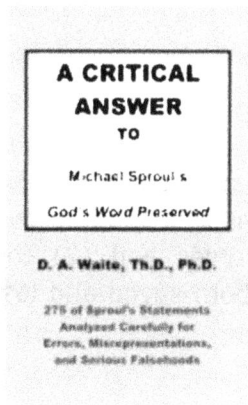

This book, *A Critical Answer to Michael Sproul's God's Word Preserved* by Dr. D. A. Waite is an attempt to bring a partial answer and reply to a number of errors and false statements in a book entitled "God's Word Preserved: A Defense of Historic Separatist Definitions and Beliefs." Dr. Waite defends the preservation, inspiration, inerrancy, and infallibility of the Words of God as promised in the Scripture, and teaches the true fundamentals about these issues. BFT #3308 for a gift of $11.00 + $5.00 S&H.

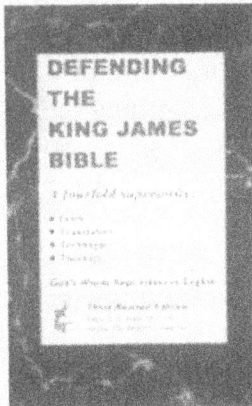

This book, *Defending The King James Bible* by Pastor D. A. Waite, Th.D., Ph.D is now a classic. It has been printed ten times through two editions. It should be in every library, school, seminary, and home. Dr. Waite's work answer's two questions: (1) Which English Bible are we to read, study, memorize, preach from, and use today? (2) Which English Bible can we hold in our hands and say with great confidence, "These are the WORDS OF GOD in English"? He examines the KING JAMES BIBLE, proving its superiority in four areas: (1) its superior TEXTS; (2) its superior TRANSLATORS; (3) its superior TECHNIQUES; and (4) its superior THEOLOGY. BFT #1594 for a gift of $12.00 + $5.00 S&H.

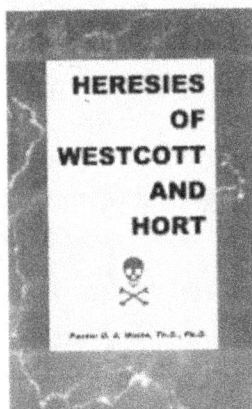

This book, *The Heresies of Westcott and Hort* by Pastor D. A. Waite, Th.D., Ph.D., is now a classic. It reveals the unorthodox beliefs of Westcott and Hort who are the men most responsible for the 'new' Greek text that underlies the 'new' bible versions. Their heterodoxy blinded their intellects, and prejudiced them adversely and unfairly in their textual theories of the Greek New Testament. This book contains 125 direct quotations of Westcott and Hort from 1,291 pages as contained in five books by both men. BFT #595 for a gift of $12.00 + $5.00 S&H

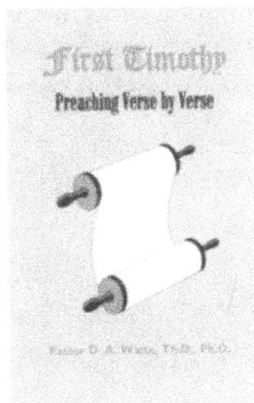

This book on First Timothy is from expository preaching sermons by Pastor D. A. Waite, Th.D., Ph.D. It brings to the mind of readers two things: (1) the meaning of the words in the verses and (2) the practical application of those words to the lives of both saved and lost people. BFT #3085 for a gift of $14.00 + $5.00 S&H.

This book on Second Timothy is the eighth in a planned series of books based on expository preaching from various books of the Bible. It is an attempt to bring to the minds of the readers two things: (1) the meaning of the words in the verses and (2) the practical application of those words to the hearts and lives of Bible-believing Christians. BFT #3105 + $5.00 S&H.

This book embraces a response to the various Fundamental institutions that share a denial that God promised and has fulfilled His promise to preserve the Hebrew, Aramaic and Greek Words which were originially given by verbal, plenary inspiration. The controversy was sparked by the publication of two books by Central Baptist Seminary, "The Bible Version Debate--The Perspective of Central Baptist Theological Seminary" and "One Bible Only?--Examining Exclusive Claims for the King James Bible." Both of these books attack the preservation of God's Words and Dr. Waite's book refutes their claim. BFT #3064 + $5.00 S&H.

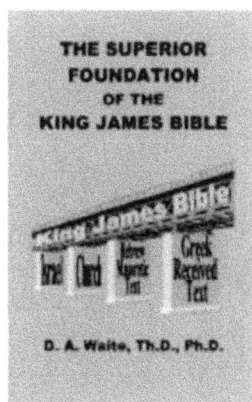

This book by Pastor D. A. Waite, Th.D., Ph.D., addresses a most important question. The question is, "Which Old Testament Hebrew and Aramaic words and which New Testament Greek Words are we to use as the basis for all of our translations"? Although it is a complex subject, Dr. Waite's book makes the topic clear for laymen, students, teacher, missionaries, and pastors. Every believer concerned about the proliferation of texts claiming to be "the Words of God" needs this book. BFT #3384 for a gift of $10.00 + $5.00 S&H.

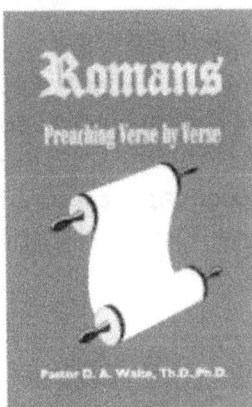

This book on Romans is from expository preaching sermons by Pastor D. A. Waite, Th.D., Ph.D. It brings to the mind of readers two things: (1) the meaning of the words in the verses and (2) the practical application of those words to the lives of both saved and lost people. BFT #2906 for a gift of $25.00 + $5.00 S&H.

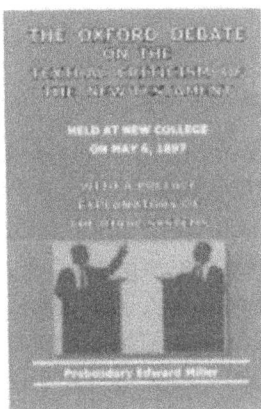

This book is the record of a debate held at Oxford University in 1897 by noted scholars of the day. Edward Miller was the assistant to Dean John William Burgon. He printed the text of the debate with the approval of the participants. The debate was about the two methods of textual criticism: (1) the method of Bishop B. F. Westcott and F. J. A. Hort, and (2) the method of Dean John William Burgon. Dean Burgon supported the Traditional Text and Westcott and Hort supported a text they constructed from two old manuscripts. BFT #3397 for a gift of $10.00 + $5.00 S&H.

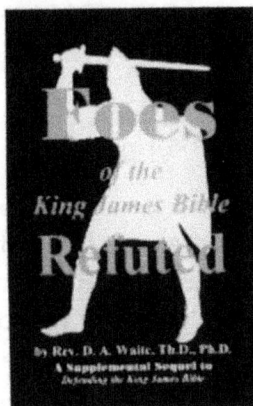

This book is important because it answers various arguments set forth by foes of the King James Bible and its underlying Hebrew, Aramaic, and Greek Texts. The arguments of the foes are not new. They have been around ever since the days of Bishop Brooke Foss Westcott and Professor Fenton John Anthony and their forerunners. Look at the principles discussed in this book, rather than at the personalities involved. BFT #2777 for a gift of $9.00 + $5.00 S&H.

Dr. Waite clearly outlines the mistakes seven fundamentalist schools are making in regard to 1. a false view of the doctrine of Bible preservation as found in the Bible, 2. their "ecumenical" and "pluralistic" approach to Bible versions. The Fundamental schools reproved and rebuked in this work reject the evidence for 356 doctrinal errors in the 'new' versions of the Bible and reject any one who uses ONLY the King James Bible. BFT #2928 for a gift of $7.00 + $5.00 S&H.

the
BIBLE
FOR
TODAY

900 Park Avenue
Collingswood, NJ 08108
Phone: 856·854-4452
www.BibleForToday.org

BFT #3418

www.ingramcontent.com/pod-product-compliance
Lightning Source LLC
Chambersburg PA
CBHW081638040426
42449CB00014B/3361